Oh, The Lessons

I've Learned!

A Redirected Me

Cheryl W. Beaufort

DEDICATION

My path has caused me to encounter so many inspirational, life changing people. None are to be forgotten. Let me extend a sincere 'Thank you' for how each of you have impacted me. I thank My Personal Savior, Jesus Christ most of all. He has been a constant and faithful Friend. I thank my husband, Bishop Harry Beaufort, for being the most important part of my life after my Lord! You have inspired, supported, encouraged, and loved me into a better place. Thank you for believing in me! This book is dedicated to you, my love!

TABLE OF CONTENTS

LIFE

Oh Life! Beautiful, ugly, mind blowing, mind bending, message sending, breath lending, Life!

She is a maze of amazing adventures and with every twist and turn, there is a lesson to be learned.

Life has been my preacher and my teacher who insisted that I leave the surface and dive a little deeper!

She coached me through childhood with great persistence.

Then stretched me into a woman with much experience!

Many times, I failed. More times, I fell. Nevertheless, I triumphed and lived to tell!

Life is filled with highs and mingled with lows, bubbling with joy, and dashed with woes.

Life has an expiration date. I never emerged to stay. But while I am here, the lessons she has taught me will never fade away.

-Cheryl W. Beaufort

INTRODUCTION

I fell to the floor before the altar in my prayer room. With my face pressed against my forearm, I wept in worship to God. His Presence was breathtaking. Suddenly, I sensed someone else in the room. I struggled to open my eyes so I could see, but I was arrested by the weight of God's Glory. His Power overwhelmed me. At that point, I surrendered. Some time had passed before I could barely open my eyes. Through the blur of tears, I saw a lady sitting beside my altar. She was beautiful. Flawless sun kissed skin blanketed her oval face. Round hazel eyes twinkled with love as they watched me then filled with tears, seeming to connect with me in worship. Gracefully, she lifted her hand towards her face as her fingers came to rest upon her chin. The sleeve which danced loosely at her wrist fell away slightly. Tattoos peeked from her inner forearm. They failed to disguise the scars underneath. As I observed her further, I noticed the changes in the texture of her hair. It was tossed back from her face exposing a fine sleek black hair line which fused into silky brown locks. However, coarse honey blonde tresses skimmed her shoulders. Thin cherry lips parted as she spoke to me. “Come on. You can do it. Get that book finished. You will write about me. When I read it, I am going to bless you with three thousand.” I woke up weeping from the vision of another angelic encounter delivering a message from Heaven’s throne.

I sat up in my bed still feeling God’s presence as I meditated on what had taken place. What would I get three thousand of? I hated waking up before I heard all I thought I should hear. I was certain however, that the angel represented women from many backgrounds and ethnicities who had experienced hardships in life. The proof of their difficulties would be the invisible scars left behind in their souls and makeshift tattoos which would attempt to mask their stories. My purpose would be to connect with those souls and through my own experiences, bring a level of healing, understanding, and show that God can redirect the life of those who may have gotten lost on their journey. Life is a phenomenal teacher and oh, the lessons I have learned.

But ye are a chosen generation, a royal priesthood, a holy nation, a peculiar people; that ye should shew forth the praises of him who hath called you out of darkness into his marvelous light.
(2 Peter 2:9 KJV)

CHAPTER 1

IT IS ALRIGHT TO BE DIFFERENT

Most mothers seem to enjoy sharing the war story of their child birthing experience with other mothers. My mom was no different, but her story about my birth sure was. Her account seemed more of a fictional tale to me until my grandmother and aunt validated it. My grandmother especially took joy in telling me the story every time we shared conversation. She constantly reminded me that I was a special child. I was not born in the sterile environment of a hospital with medically trained baby doctors and nurses rallying around my mom. She gave birth to me in the back of a small four room board house she called home. Her support team was my dad, Grandma Lou, Grandma Sophie, Aunt Ruby, and an old midwife named Ms. Catherine who delivered many of the babies in the community. I am sure most expectant moms approach labor and delivery with a great deal of anxiety. My mom's level of nervousness had to be amplified because she had lost a son and daughter before me. My sister, Angela was a stillborn. Life was snatched from her 5 minutes before she entered the world. My brother, Willie, died within 24 hours of being born. Mama heard him cry all night but never got a chance to see him. My dad came to her bedside the next day to tell her that their son did not make it. So, I was mama's third attempt. The old phrase says, 'the third time's a charm'. It was true in my mom's case. Not only did I emerge strong and healthy, God gave me life to break the cycle of death plaguing my mother. My first cry prophesied that her life had shifted from tragedy to triumph.

My birth was unusual. Many of the bizarre details shared with me by my mom and grandmother remain branded into my mind. For instance, I was the first baby Ms. Catherine, the midwife, had ever delivered facing up. Grandma recalled how startled Ms. Catherine was to see my infant face with opened eyes looking back at her. In 1970, that was not heard of much in our rural area. Grandma Lou said I came out watching with a double veil over my face. She described a small white, thin web which rested over each of my eyes and a larger one carefully laid so it covered my entire face. My grandma said she watched as the midwife lifted the veil from my face to reveal intriguing almond shaped, oriental eyes with pitch black pupils peering back at the them both. Mama remembered being frightened by my piercing stares. She said when I was only a few days old, my eyes would follow her around the room as if I was watching her every move. She explained that I had snake like eyes which seem to look deep inside of her. She grew apprehensive about breastfeeding for that reason. She recalled the many times I would be looking at her as I fed from her breast and suddenly, my forehead would wrinkle, my gaze intensified, and I would latch down on her breast harder as if I was biting her. I found it hilarious when she divulged that at times, she expected a fork like tongue to stick out from my mouth and strike her. Mama said her tension did not subside until my grandmother explained I was just incredibly wise and was in a sense, studying her. She told me she adopted the practice of soothing me with kisses to my forehead which always caused a smile to creep across my lips.

Also, I was told that as I emerged from my mother, the strong fragrance of flowers filled the room, and everyone present acknowledged it. Mama associated the smell to fresh gardenias. The midwife declared I was going to be a unique child because she had never witnessed such a delivery in any of her years of experience. However, fear struck in my mom's heart when my Grandma Sophie blurted out that I was a *root baby*, indicating that my life would be connected to sorcery. I wished many days that those words were never shared with me.

As I grew, peculiarity continued to follow me. Yet, Grandma Lou would attribute what I considered "strange" as "a gift". When I was about 3 years old, I can remember sleep walking. At least, that is what my parents called it. My favorite sleeping position was on my side with my face towards the wall. I kept my back turned to the door, and away from the eeriness of the pitch-dark room. Night always scared me. While sleeping, I could hear a voice calling my name. Drowsily, I would open my eyes, and marvel because I could see through the wall. There would be a tall thin man making his way down the long murky dirt road which led to our home. He had a distinctive walk. Long slow strides moved him closer and closer. As he approached, I could hear him whistling an unfamiliar tune. His jingle was only interrupted when he stopped to call my name. When he reached the front porch, he would toss back the tail of his dark unbuttoned coat, take a seat on the porch's edge, and remove his small brim hat. As if he knew I was watching, he would turn towards my bedroom window and motion for me to come outside. Although I did not recognize the man, something was hauntingly familiar about him. There was an unexplainable connection, hypnotic almost, which seemed to draw me when he called. His presence lured me beyond my fear of the dark. I would crawl out of bed and shuffle through the blackness of my room on to our front door. The old barrel bolt lock was no match for my determination. Yet, as soon as I pried the latch from its hold, the clank of the metal always sounded an alarm to stir mama and daddy from their sleep. I could hear the scuffle of their feet moving towards me. One of them would shovel me up and carry me back to bed. This became a repetitive event.

One morning, my parents finally sat me down and questioned me about my nocturnal behavior. As I shared the details, they stared at me with disbelief. But as I gave the description of the man, mama and daddy's facial expressions changed. Shock swept my mama's face. Daddy's eyes filled with tears as he suddenly walked out the door. I gazed at mama for answers. She explained that I had just described my deceased grandfather. That day, I found out that my grandfather died before my first birthday. My grandfather refused to hold any babies, including his own. He had to judge them "big enough" first. Yet, he chose to hold me as an infant. I was the first infant he ever held. Many days, my grandfather would make his way to our home, take a seat on the edge of our front porch and holler into the house for my mama to bring me to him. Mama shared with me how he would hold me in his arms and whistle for a while. Then he would talk to me. She said one day, granddaddy handed me back to her and told her to always watch out for me because I was special and wise. Not long after, my grandfather died of a heart attack in my dad's arms as he was being rushed to the hospital. Following that conversation with my mama, I never saw my grandfather again. However, I did continue to see. I saw angels and demons. I saw horses and horsemen. Paranormal became my normal and silence became my choice.

When I was old enough to start school, I was plagued severely with separation anxiety. I cried every day. I played alone. Nobody wanted to be my friend and I was too shy to ask. One day, I was sitting by myself on the playground hoping that someone would come and befriend me. No one did. I was sure most of them labeled me "the weird girl". My attention was drawn to one little girl who came running pass me. As I stared at her, my head told me that her name was Susan. I questioned if that were true because

I had never met her. She was not in my class. Curiosity won the argument and I had to find out. Against the warning inside of me, I called out the name Susan. I was amazed when she stopped running and turned to walk toward me. I smiled at her with great hopes that my days of being friendless were over. Disappointment shattered my smile when she gave me a dirty look and asked me how I knew her name. In honesty, I told her that I did not know how I knew, I just did, and I wanted to be her friend. She shoved me to the ground and shouted at me! She said I had better not ever call her name again because I was a stupid girl and she would never be my friend. The gift had betrayed me. Hope left me ashamed. That was my first encounter with rejection and the pain of it settled into the wound of my soul. From that moment, I derived that I was only safe with myself. Although my heart secretly desired to be accepted by others, my mind convinced me that I was better off alone.

Dreams and visions became commonplace in my life. A rare wisdom rested on me throughout my childhood. Although I knew things no normal child my age might have, I did not fully view myself as abnormal. Others may have thought that about me, but I did not think it about myself until a conversation convinced me. One day, my mom went to the old country store in our community to put gas in our car. I ran inside to pay for it and get some penny candies with the coins I picked up from around. The lady behind the counter helped me count out the candy. As she handed me the bulging brown paper sack, she told me that I was a special little girl and I was going to be just like my grandmother and help a lot of people. I told her thank you as I raced out the store. I heard her words, but thoughts of fruit chews and tootsie rolls chased them from my mind. A few days later, two little girls approached me on the playground at recess. One said her mama warned her not to play with me because my grandma was a bad woman. I retorted I loved my grandma and she was not a bad woman. The little girl mockingly said my grandma was a root woman and she was not going to mess with me because I might tell my grandma to make her die. Those words taunted me for days. I decided to talk to my grandma about the incident. She explained that some people have extraordinary gifts. They can see into the future to learn things about others then use that information to help them. She said those individuals were called *helpers*. She continued sharing that some people, like root women, use their gift to hurt others. She said she was not a *root woman*, but *a helper*. I heard her explanation, but the little girl's words from the playground resonated louder inside of me. I began to watch more closely. I saw strange people come and go at my grandma's house. My uncles and aunts started referring to them as *"company*". They would come inside and disappear behind the beaded curtain which concealed the front room. One day, nosiness got the best of me. I peeped into the room to see what was so secretive. My grandmother saw me and called me inside. I was hesitant. Uneasiness warned me to leave but intrigue drew me in. The room seemed unnervingly cold and dark. A small wooden table was nested in front of the only window in the room. Thick red curtains fought to keep out the only chance of light. Grandma was seated on one side of the table. A young woman was sitting nervously on the other side. The table held an old silver percolator and chipped white coffee cup. Grandma poured a smidge of coffee into the cup and told the lady to take a sip. The lady sipped and placed the cup back on the table. Grandma heisted the window, dashed the remaining coffee out and gazed into the bottom of the cup. She motioned for me to come over to her. In an unusual hushed tone, grandma instructed me to examine the cup and tell the lady what I saw. I peered inside the cup and whispered, 'I see coffee'. Grandma chided me and said to look deeper, pass the coffee and tell her what I saw. I watched for a moment and images began to form. Before I could distinguish any of them, I instinctively closed my eyes and said I did not see anything. Grandma scolded me! She said she knew I saw something, and I was being stubborn. She swatted my back side and told me to go outside and play. As I wandered out into the yard, my insides trembled. I knew something was terribly wrong with what I had witnessed. Although I had lied to my grandma, a sense of satisfaction deeper inside of me told me I did the right thing. In that moment I began to entertain the possibility. Maybe my grandma was a 'root woman'. I wondered if what the old lady said in the store was true. Was I really going to be like my grandmother? I grew determined to never let that happen. If the dreams, visions, and knowledge made me strange like her, then I would stop it all and be normal like everybody else. In the years that followed, I worked diligently to be the best unnoticed version of normal imaginable but lost my true self in the process. As much as I preferred to be the chameleon in the background, there was a captive locked inside of my soul crying loud for release. However, I turned a deaf ear in hopes of silencing her pleas. Because I could not see the beauty of my own uniqueness, all I wanted to do was disappear among the masses of ordinary people. I discovered that it is not so easy to fit in when you have been chosen to stand out.

I remember many carefree days growing up. Although God had a plan for my life that I did not fully comprehend, I did not worry myself with any of the details. I spent many days lying on a blanket of green grass trying to make out the shapes of clouds.

Maybe my ignorance was bliss! Afterall, I often heard adults say about children, "Child, they don't know no better"! Or maybe, my life was being ordered by simplistic, child-like faith. Rather it was ignorance or child-like faith, I was moving towards my predestined purpose until I was redirected by rejection. I was comfortable in my own skin before I allowed the words of another mortal to have more influence in my life than the words of my Creator. As I got older, self-rejection evolved. I began to look at who I was with disdain. I realize that I did what should NEVER be done. I came into agreement with the spirit of rejection.

The spirit of rejection spun thoughts in my mind which told me that I did not have friends because nobody wanted me around. I would never be good enough for anyone to choose me for their kickball team. I was too weird for the 4H club. I missed many opportunities which came before me because rejection would always convince me that I did not fit. This destructive lie followed me from the primary playground to the halls of high school. At first, I alienated myself and did all I could to be quiet and unseen in a desperate attempt to avoid the pain of rejection again. Around the tenth grade, I morphed into the role of a people pleaser without even realizing it. Although my vulnerability often left me used, I would agree to do whatever would breed approval and acceptance. It was not long before my life seemed swallowed up by acting. I would switch into character and portray whatever part seemed necessary. In the process, I fell victim to identity crisis. I lost touch with who I was called to be. Around the twelfth grade, I had embraced a false persona and began impersonating someone who had it all together. But deep inside, I was spiritually lost! When I was alone in bed at night, that haunting thought would materialize before me. No matter how I tried to dismiss it, the truth was I had opted to cleave to a counterfeit design of myself because the original me was too intimidating. Many nights, I cried myself to sleep. I could feel the tug of God reminding me of how far I had drifted from Him. Yet, I would get up the next day and play the game of charades all over again.

Well into my adult life, I began to figure out that the enemy wanted me to fear being an oddity in the earth. He used the spirit of rejection to execute that plot. For many years, I fell for it. I developed a misconception that being a unique creation of God and submitting my life to His will made me look bizarre. For me, that was unacceptable. As a result, I deviated from my ordained path. When I resisted God's way, I became open game for the enemy. Sinful desires baited me, curiosity bound me, and indulgence led me straight into a pit of regrets. Emotionally and spiritually, I found myself in a cold dark place. After a while, I began to yearn for the peace that I once knew as a child. Once again, I wanted to experience the joy of innocence I had before the wicked wiles of the enemy touched me. I recalled the sense of satisfaction which overflowed from the depths of my spirit when I walked in obedience to God. I craved it. In retrospect, there was a time when I embraced what I needed but did not know how to appreciate it. What is unappreciated is eventually lost.

As I pondered over all the poor decisions which got me in that place of reflections and despair, I realized that I was like the Prophet Jonah in the bible. I did not want to go where God was sending me. I did not want the mission. Although I tried to avoid looking crazy to others, I found myself looking crazy to me. One day, through the silence of my weariness, I heard a familiar voice cry out. I thought she would have died after so much time had elapsed, but my true self had awakened. Despite how I tried to stifle her cries with denial or bury her purpose with uncertainty, she once again discovered her voice and demanded release. Fortunately, I did not dismiss her pleas. I decided to return to God's original design for my life and no longer shun the woman I was destined to become. However, my decision did not create the change overnight. I had work to do. I had to accept responsibility for my actions. My choice to go contrary to the will of God in the first place left me laden with layers of guilt, regret, and consequences I needed to sort through. I still struggled with people's perception of me. At times, my thoughts convince me that I was too strange to be accepted. As much as I wanted to start over with God, and rebuild our relationship, I was apprehensive about the outcome. What if I began only to discover that I lacked the tenacity to keep going when challenges showed up? Among the many battles raging within me, the biggest battle was the fear of rejection from those I was being built for. Many times, I was determined to become a trailblazer, but no sooner than zeal would burn within me, thoughts of being cast aside would douse my fire. One day, I was so frustrated with myself for the inability to move beyond such a mindset. I knew I should have been pass that but for some reason, I felt stuck. I was in deep thought seeking a solution when I was struck by an epiphany.

I had always been mesmerized by the unusual details surrounding my birth. But my differences began long before the story was told. Upon conception, God created a unique liner inside of my mother's uterus called a placenta which housed me and grew as I did. The placenta worked to deliver essential nutrients to my body as well as eliminate any waste that may have been present. Once I was delivered, the job of the placenta was complete, so it passed from mother's body after I did. There was a remarkable difference between the uterus and the placenta. Even though my mother's uterus could be reused to bring forth my sisters which came after me, the placenta could not. I believe the placenta operated under natural orders from God. Therefore, my body received vital nutrition to ensure proper development. Simultaneously, the placenta was under supernatural command. Specific qualities had to be implanted within my soul to form my personality. Exclusive traits were embedded in my DNA to establish my individuality. Divine gifts were transported into my spirit to equip me with a distinctive spirituality. God left his imprint upon the blueprint of who I would become and gave me everything required for success. He wrapped me with uniqueness and commanded the placenta to let me marinate in all of it until my release. Upon delivery, the placenta's purpose was over because it was designed specifically for me. No one else could come forth from it. I arrived as a divine design. God creates only originals. No duplicates. From the day of that revelation, I began to accept my differences and embrace my authenticity with a newfound appreciation.

It took a while, but I finally realized that I was a premeditated work of God's hands and so are you! Let us not waste time focusing on what we consider imperfections. The size and shape of our bodies, the color of our hair or the shades of our skin have no bearing on our God given purpose. Mistakes from our past or family history does not have the power to define our future unless we give permission. As a matter of a fact, all our experiences may be what qualified us for where we are going. We can no longer afford to be so discontent with ourselves and exchange the true essence of who God says we are for an image of what we deem better. It is so easy to get caught up in the '*if only*' of life. *If only I was taller and thinner. If only my hair was longer, straighter, or curlier. If only I was smarter or braver. If only I could have been reared under different circumstances.* When God created us, He destroyed the mold. That speaks volumes about our originality. We must value and embrace our differences and be proud of them. We are not unacceptable. We are necessary. The bible speaks of believers as being *peculiar*. Most people relate that word with being strange, uncommon, or odd. When the word is used in the bible, specifically in 1 Peter 2:9 King James Version, it translates from the Greek word *peripoiesis* which means to completely obtain, acquire, make one's own, become the special possession of, preserved for one's self. Our differences are God's trademark that we are His! Before this revelation, I grieved over my perceived differences. Now that I know better, I live better.

Beloved, let me speak personally to you. The forces of darkness do not want you to live out your God given purpose. They would much rather have you cemented to your failures or fixated upon everything you dislike about your life. Instead, see your greatness. Imagine where you could be or how far you could go and get determined to persevere beyond any objection that may arise. Take the time to appreciate every unusual trait or strange quirk that makes you distinctive. Embrace every magical memory or awe-inspiring moment that helped build the peculiar you. You are not like anyone else in this world. You are uniquely, unequivocally you and no one will ever be better at it. You are different and guess what? It is alright!

Redirected from the fear of being different!

I consider that our present sufferings are not worth comparing with the glory that will be revealed in us.
(Romans 8:18 NIV)

CHAPTER 2

GOD WANTS GLORY FROM EVERY PLATFORM

The dismissal bell rang! Mrs. Kennedy, our third-grade teacher, was posted at the door of our class. Everyone grabbed their books and dashed pass her into the flood of students in the hallway. I tried to get up from my desk, but something was wrong. My legs were tingling. I managed to push pass the strange sensation, grabbed my books, and headed outside to the bus. The walk seemed like it was taking forever this time. My bus was waiting. I could hear Mrs. Kennedy shouting for me to hurry but I could not. My brain may have been sending the signal that I needed to move quicker, but my legs were not getting the message. From out of nowhere, someone scooped me up, carried me to my bus and sat me on the front seat. When the school bus got to my stop, everyone got off except for me. My legs felt like heavy weights. Mr. King, our bus driver, looked back at me. I was always very shy and did not talk much. But I answered his glare by telling him my legs would not work. He told me that I needed to get off the bus. He did not know I was being serious. I held on to the bars at the front door of the bus and pulled myself up, but when I tried to go down the steps to exit the bus, my legs failed to move. I fell. My uncle, Eddie, helped me from the door of the bus. People were yelling. I was terrified! The thought to cry came to my mind but fear and confusion rushed it away. I did not know what was happening to me. I was only seven years old. The day before I was running and playing! Within 24 hours, I was paralyzed.

The events unfolded quickly from there. I was admitted into McLeod Hospital in Florence, SC. Doctors and nurses filled my bedside trying to find a diagnosis, but the mystery remained unsolved. My condition grew worse. I was transported to the

Children's Hospital at Medical University of South Carolina in Charleston, S.C. By the time I reached there, paralysis had progressed from my legs to my entire body. I could only turn my head from one side to the other. After many blood tests, the doctors diagnosed me with Guillain Barre Syndrome although I do not think they were certain. As frightening as my situation was, I found myself crying more for the little girl in the bed beside me who was burned severely. The more she cried out in pain, the more I cried for her wishing somebody could do something to help. Then one day, I woke up and she was no longer in the room. One of the nurses said she was transferred. I was left alone, afraid, and full of questions, but I never contemplated dying. Of all the thoughts that came to me during my moments of solitude, death never entered my mind. Even when the doctors spoke it, my spirit rejected it. The bible said that all sickness was not unto death, but for the glory of God to be revealed! God was about to use me to prove it!

I remember seeing the look of horror on my mama's face when the doctors told her my chances of survival were slim to none and if I did survive, I would be in a vegetative state for the rest of my life. Anyone with common sense who looked at my set of circumstances would have been inclined to believe the doctor's report. I must have looked so frail lying there surrounded by machines, wires, and tubes. My nutrition came through tubes. Tubes helped me to breathe. I had strange contraptions on my hands and feet that the nurses called splints. They were support devices designed to keep my limbs from twisting and withering. To many, I am sure my end looked certain. I never suspected that the stage had to be set in such a way because God was getting ready to manifest His power in my life. I was about to learn not to look on dire circumstances and draw a negative conclusion when God is in the equation.

One day, mama came to visit me and brought a new testament that my grandmother sent. She opened it and put it under my pillow. My grandmother instructed her to leave the bible there. She told me that my grandmother wanted me to talk to Jesus. I had not thought of talking to Jesus prior to her saying it, but afterwards, those words kept ringing in my head. Several days later, I was lying in my bed late at night. The hospital halls were quiet. I remembered the little bible under my pillow and the words of my grandmother. I wrestled with the thought of having a conversation with someone I could not see. Sure, I heard people talk about Jesus, but I had never seen Him. Nevertheless, my thoughts were overtaken by a strong urge to talk to Him and see if He would show up. Before I could utter a word, something very strange happened. I am not sure if I had a vision, a dream or the events occurred. I am certain that what transpired was real enough to leave a lasting impression in my memory.

A very tall black man wearing a long black trench coat and brim hat walked into my room carrying a large black bag. He placed the bag at the foot of my bed. I spoke to him, but he said nothing. He just opened the bag and took out a small jar. He took the top off the jar, reached inside, and threw some dust over my bed that fell upon me like glitter. He closed the jar, placed it back in the bag, grabbed the bag and walked out of my room never even making eye contact with me. I was horrified! The terror grew when I knew he walked out the door, but I never saw him go down the hall! It was like he disappeared. In that moment, I realized I needed someone watching out for me. Mama could not be there to protect me. She had my sister and dad that needed her attention at home and even at such an early age, I understood that. If there was a time to try Jesus, like my grandmother suggested, I had found it. I told Jesus that I believed in Him and I knew He was with me and was not going to let anything bad happen to me. Strangely, I found peace and went on to sleep. The very next morning, a nurse was passing my room door as I felt the need to stretch. She saw when my leg lifted so she dashed into the room. The next thing I knew, the room was flooded by doctors! One doctor asked me to stretch again, but I could not. He patted my feet and said it was alright. It had to be alright, I thought. I felt the doctor's touch, but I was too shy to say so. I just rested in knowledge that something happened in my body. Not long after that, I was sent to a crippled children's home in Turbeville, SC. My third-grade teacher would come and read lessons to me. She would write my answers because I was still paralyzed in some areas with severe muscle weakness in others. I was confined to the bed, so the nurses fed me, washed me, and brought me a bed pan to use the bathroom. One Sunday, I watched the children from the window in my room as they ran around tagging each other on the playground. I longed to be outside with them. I looked up at the ceiling and prayed. "Jesus, if You will let me run and play like the other children, I will be a good girl for You, and I will do whatever You want me to do." God answered that simple, sincere prayer. It appears Heaven was waiting on that announcement from my lips! I believe my declaration initiated a breakthrough!

Immediately, my room was filled with such a bright light! I looked back at the window to the playground, but the view had changed. An angel was standing in front of the window. He was enormous! The bright light that surrounded him was unlike any light I had ever seen before. I tried to see his face but looking into his face was like staring into the sun. The glare hurt my eyes. The angel was draped in a pristine white garment gathered at the waist with a wide gold band. The sheer material seemed to dance in a breeze of wind that I did not feel. Long golden strands of hair flowed from behind the brightness of his face. I stared speechless at his massive white wings. No words were verbalized. The conversation was through our thoughts. The angel was telling me to get up and walk. I was telling the angel that I could not because I had been that way for a long time. Yet, something greater inside of me yearned at the possibility of walking again. Suddenly, a hot sensation sat on my forehead and began to spread to my toes. It felt like someone was slowly pouring slightly uncomfortable hot water all over me. Before I realized anything else, I was sitting on the side of my bed. Then, in amazement, I stood trembling! I wanted to touch the angel. I walked a great distance across the floor to the angel, but before my hand could reach him, he disappeared. I turned around and could not believe how far I had walked. It had been such a long time. I made my way back to my bed, crawled in and pulled my covers up over me all the time trying to decide if what happened was real. A nurse came in to check on me. I told her that I wanted to go home. She said I could not go home until I could walk. Her comment stirred the heat of indignation inside of me. I threw the covers back and got out of the bed. She began to cry and call Jesus. She told me to get back in bed and she would call my mom. Soon the nurse returned to the room to notify me that she was unable to reach my mom but would keep trying. Just as I started to cry, my mom and dad rushed in the door. Mama had tears in her eyes and fear on her face for some reason. She asked if I was alright. I told her that I could walk, and I wanted to go home. My parents stood there looking at me in disbelief. I eased my way out of bed to prove to them something mind blowing had happened to me! As I stood, my mom cried hysterically! That time, the tears were not worry, they were praise! The doctor came in later to examine me. He said I was in remission, but it was only temporary. The paralysis would return. Against the doctor's advice, my mom and dad took me home that day! On the drive home, mom and dad explained to me that my grandmother was in church at the altar praying for me and passed out. While unconscious, she had a vision of me levitating over my bed as my clothes transformed into a white robe. When she came out of the vision, she sent someone to tell my parents they needed to hurry and get to me. My grandmother thought I had transitioned from life to death. My mom ran into my room not knowing what to expect which explained the look of fear on her face. The unexpected had happened. I had become the recipient of a miracle! The healing power of God destroyed the bands of affliction which held me. Regardless of what my doctor's medical training taught him, I was not in remission. I was in full recovery.

When I took time as an adult to reflect on the set of circumstances which led to my miracle, I gained great understanding. As a little girl, I was struck by adversity that I, nor my parents, ever saw coming. Yet, God got glory out of it. If I was not placed in that situation, I may have never reached for Jesus when I did. Beloved, that is a lesson to glean! God can cause contrary circumstances to yield unexpected results! Sometimes, we must be pushed into the corner with our back against a wall before change erupts. Situations strike to provoke us to reach for Jesus. Moments of hardship arise to motivate us to move forward. Adversity can operate as the catalyst for advancement! Even when life brings difficulty, God desires glory!

The tall dark stranger which entered my room was an encounter with the power of darkness. Hell was on assignment to lay claim to my life. The power of darkness wanted rights to my miracle. A face to face encounter with an agent from hell was enough to persuade me that I needed the protection of God in my life. Affliction was my opportunity to cry out in a petition to God and witness results. I became convinced that Jesus was real, and prayer worked. I experienced firsthand, the miracle working power of God. For that reason, I did not have time to bemoan what happened to me. I became too grateful to be grudgeful.

At some point in life, everybody gets hit with the unexpected. Some matters are only normal occurrences, while others may be caused by someone's negligence or ignorance. In some cases, situations are self-inflicted. People find themselves blindsided by the consequences of their own poor decisions. Conditions are made worse when a personal moment becomes a public matter. In society, misfortunes seldom remain a secret. Even as a young child, I learned what it felt like to be a public spectacle during the days of my health challenges. Medical professionals were always around me poking and prodding. Random people disregarded privacy statutes as they walked in and out of my hospital room for no apparent reason. Many people in our community knew about my affliction. People do talk in small towns, so I know my family and I were the subject of many conversations. I am sure some prayed for us while others may have been expecting to hear that I had died. Even though I could not comprehend it at the time, God was working His plan for my life. I have learned to call times where it seems like everybody knows your business **predestined**

platforms. The word *predestined* reminded me that God knew what would happen before it unfolded, therefore, he maintained control of the outcome. *Platforms* are raised or elevated places. Whoever is on the platform is easily seen by spectators around them. When God allows your life to be highly visible to others, there is purpose behind it.

Apostle Clavon Leonard once told me that God knows how to set the stage to get the best out of you. I found that to be the absolute truth in my life. Many times, I was made to feel like a half dressed, unprepared performer pushed on to the platform while my most personal moments were being exposed. However, what I thought were the worst roles anyone could be expected to play turned out to be golden opportunities to glean from the experience, gather strategies and gain an inner strength. Let me admit to you that I was not always the heroine. Many times, I had to recover from defeat. You see, enduring the process God uses to build and equip is not easy. However, with perseverance, you may discover that it will work for your good. It took some time, but after a while, I was skilled enough to land the leading role as an award-winning overcomer in the screenplay of my life. One day, I realized that I was not "an extra" thrown into a scene. I was carefully selected for the part and my victory was written into the script.

Maybe you have experienced some moments that left you riddled with disappointment, guilt, or shame. Perhaps you may have found yourself in the grip of regret over some poor decision you made. Possibly, you were victimized by someone who handled you irresponsibly. Life could have dealt you a bad hand and daily, you have struggled to play it to the best of your ability. Perchance, it all unfolded on a public platform and you are trying to recover from the degradation of everybody knowing your business. I understand the embarrassment sometimes associated with being a public display. I can relate to the poor posture of a broken spirit being exhibited from the platform. Shame creates bowed down heads and slumped shoulders. Backs become bent with the weight of uncertainty. Faith takes such a beating; it can no longer sustain an erect stance. Spiritual slouching occurs. I am all too familiar with living moments I wished were just nightmares that I could wake up from and it would be over. In my life, the platform has proven itself to be a stern teacher. Of its many lessons, I discovered that platforms were created for people to *stand* on. *How* a person stands determines the fail or the pass. Even the definition of stand hints at how to pass the test of the platform. From the Oxford and Merriam Webster's Dictionaries, I concluded that **stand** means to *become firmly fixed* in a place and *maintain an upright position supported by one's feet*. This means the platform is not the place to pass out. Instead, you should focus on three words: **feet, faith, and favor**. Whether you have been summoned to the platform of life or hurled on to it through unfortunate circumstances, it is vital to remain firmly fixed. To me, that means you must focus on the position of your feet and your faith while ignoring the urge to run. If you run, you will miss the lesson! No, running is not the option you should choose. Standing is! When I stand on something, by faith, I believe it will support me. In addition, my faith tells me I am standing on something that is subject to me because it is under my feet. Once I gain the understanding that I have authority in the matter, and God has control of the matter, then uncertainty must leave the stage. Doubt and fear must exit left. It is all about perception! If you can perceive that you have power over the platform and the platform does not have power over you, then you can overcome the challenges it brings.

Another word used in the definition of stand was *upright*. Upright can be used to describe a person who is honorable because he or she holds fast to strong morals and lives according to sound principles. The opposite of upright is crooked and dishonorable. Not only are the innocent called to the platform, the guilty are too. Sometimes, people find themselves on the platform before others because they refuse to walk upright. Dishonest ways drag them to the platform for exposure with hope seated in the balcony believing the behavior will change. If these were your terms, then make up your mind to walk upright. Divorce dishonesty. Let me share this word of wisdom with you. It does not make sense to seek a divorce from anything you deny being married to.

Acknowledgement is key. First, you must recognize wrong ways before you can overcome them. Upright ways will bring the favor of God upon your life. Proverbs 16:7 in the Christian Standard Bible Version says *When a person's ways please the Lord, He makes even his enemies to be at peace with him.* Strive to be the type of individual who walks with such integrity until your mere presence hails respect, even when encompassed by enemies. Then work to maintain upright ways.

Please understand that the same platform used to display the negative, can also unveil the great. In my experiences, God acquainted me with the platform, not to leave me ashamed and broken before people. He chose my life to reveal His power, ability to restore, deliver and heal. I am so honored and humbled that God picked me as a little girl to be a witness for Him. Something beyond explanation transpired within me when God used the platform of paralysis to unveil a miracle. The same power which lifted me from a state of paralysis can stand you up and move you pass anything determined to cripple or hinder you.

Even if a negative thing called you to the platform, a positive thing could usher you from it. You may have encountered many failures, disappointments, heartbreaks, tragedies, and loss in life, but the sufferings will never compare to the glory God desires to reveal in you. Glory is defined by such words as brightness, splendor, greatness, and honor. Regardless of life's adversity, it is important to remember that God wants to replace what brought you dishonor with what will bring you honor. He desires to transform your darkest moments of defeat into your brightest moments of victory. Endure the platform. Do not dismiss the lessons weaved throughout the experience. Believe that God is with you every step of the way and let your story reveal His glory.

Redirected from the paralysis of public attention!

"For there is no one so great or mighty that he can avoid the misery that will rise up against him when he resists and strives against God" -John Calvin

CHAPTER 3

REBELLION HAS A HIDDEN PRICE TAG

I stood at the front door with bag in hand and hollered back into the dining room, "Mama, don't make me choose!" Mama stood there looking at me in disbelief while Don, my high school sweetheart, stood in the yard waiting. For a fleeting moment, I hesitated. I was standing between what felt like my past and my future. Separating the two was an old rickety metal frame door with glass panes barely holding on. I struggled against the dated door latch. The winds grabbed the door and slung it wide open adding to my dramatic exit! Clumsily, I dropped my bag. Reaching down to get it, I heard the door crash against the metal of our double wide mobile home. I snatched up my bag and stood to see the door rushing back at me. BAM! It slammed in my face. Startled, I once again fought the door latch until I broke free dashing down the steps and onto the car. I opened the passenger back door and tossed in my bag. The car door closed with a loud thump. I could feel mama watching me from the front door of the house, but I fought the impulse to look. I wrestled with the car's front door and slung myself into the passenger seat. When I looked over, Don was still standing in the door of the driver's side. One foot was in the floor of the car while the other rested on the ground. He stood there seemingly lost by the whirlwind of confusion going on around him. My sharp tone broke his stare. "Come on! What are you waiting on? Let's go and let's go now!" I demanded. Against my determination not to, my eyes glanced up at mama standing in the doorway.

"Sherry, please don't do it! You gonna regret it. You got time Sherry, please!" Mama pleaded. The hurt in her eyes cut into the cold anger of my heart, but pride quickly fought back my tears.

Ignoring her, I snuffed at Don. "Let's go I said!" Don sank down into the driver's seat. The sound of the door closing shook the reality of what I was doing in my mind. As Don and I rode down the dirt road from my house, the arrogance of my proven point was lost in the dust behind us. Conviction arose within me as my conscience told me I was in error. Thoughts of right and wrong continued to grapple with each other in my mind. I realized I had never spoken to mama like that. I knew she loved me! I was convinced she would only tell me what was best for me. But why could she not understand where I was? I was in love. Why could she not accept Don as my choice for my future? Her face appeared before me again. I remembered the heartbreak in her eyes as tears fell from my own then tumbled down my cheeks. "God, help me. How did I get here?" I whispered in my mind. I sat straight up in the bed! God would use dreams to warn me or instruct me! The problem was my refusal to heed!

During the time of the dream, I was a senior in high school. I had a car and was making good grades. I had a few friends. I even had a high school sweetheart that I was head over heels for. I know longer thought of myself as an ugly duckling. I recall writing my five-year goal in my High School yearbook! My plans were to finish college with my nursing degree, land an excellent job in a hospital and prepare to buy or build my own upstairs home in a nice country setting. However, I got so distracted by my relationship with Don, I neglected my relationship with God. Don's voice and desires had more influence on me than the Lord. Therefore, pleasing my idol quickly became my new priority. I wanted to go to Claflin University in Orangeburg SC after high school to pursue my nursing degree, but when Don did not agree, I compromised and began attending USC-Sumter SC. Because that was not my true heart's desire, I did well but did not stay long. Please understand, compromise will never bring true fulfillment.

I found it strange when I went back to read my five- year vision a few years after I wrote it and discovered that Don's name was never written in it. Somehow, I had unconsciously or God-consciously omitted him. His name was nowhere on the page. Yet, two years after high school, I married him. Instead of college, I began working to make money and my five-year vision for my future got lost among the cases of shoes I unpacked at Walmart. I had potential but lost pursuit, so regret became my reality. I loathed the place I found myself in. I knew the bible said with every temptation, God would make a way of escape! I desperately hoped the same would apply to a tough situation, especially a self-inflicted one. Although I was in urgent need of a way out, I felt like my life was stuck on repeat. Looking for answers, I began to replay that dream I had over and over in my mind. It was like punishment, but I was trying to make sense of how I got so far off course from my goals and aspirations.

My dream was God's counsel which I chose to ignore. For instance, in the dream, I hesitated momentarily when I was standing at the door. Doors often symbolize opportunities. Although an opportunity is presented, that does not mean it should be hastily accepted. Every door is not the right door. Some matters are better left untampered with. If I had taken the time to observe, I might have understood the signs of uncertainty and unreliable perception ahead of me symbolized by the windowpanes which were barely attached. I believe the moment of hesitation was the reigns of my conscience pulling me away from a wrong decision. Right then, I was afforded the opportunity to seek and embrace the leading of God before I walked through the door. Instead, emotions seized the moment. As I wrestled with the old latch, God may have been telling me to think about my next step again, but my fleshly desire dismissed the thought. At that moment, I became emotionally driven when I should have been spiritually led. Oftentimes, we force open doors God never intended for us to cross the threshold of because we are emotionally driven to do so. Emotions easily cloud sound judgement. The voice of wisdom coming from the mouth of my mom was warning me that regret stems from reckless choices. The look of disappointment upon her face, the hurt in her eyes and the pleas coming from her heart illustrated how I must have made God feel knowing that I was getting ready to embrace a life far beneath what was planned for me. I heard collisions in my future when the door crashed against the house's exterior and returned to slam shut in my face. Walking through wrong doors, or right doors in wrong seasons, can cause unnecessary confrontations. For example, marriage was an ordained door for me. However, I walked through it prematurely. Therefore, I met with unnecessary heartache. Just like the front door that slammed shut in my face, many ideas crashed before me and windows of opportunities abruptly closed before I could get through. I had to acknowledge that some of those disappointments were consequences of my disobedience. My struggle to get the front door of the car opened in the dream may have symbolized God attempting to block me from sitting in a seat of rebellion. I resisted His intervention in the dream and brought that behavior into my conscious existence as well.

Failure to yield to God's way became a pattern in my life. Every time I did so, I opened another door for opposition to walk in and take a seat. Thinking back to the dream, I wrestled to open the car's front door before I could get in. I believe that was an indication of how I would ignorantly fight for front seats of rebellion in exchange for some great places God had reserved for me. Void of God's counsel, I made my own decisions which led me down a path far more challenging than it had to be. Even in rare instances when I found myself at a state of peace and joy, I would self- sabotage by giving into the pull of my emotions and desires which were contrary to the leading of the Holy Spirit. Just like in the dream, the Holy Spirit was always moving on my heart to help me do the right thing. He was like the flagman trying to direct me away from danger, but all too often, I refused to heed. Throughout my life, God did his best to direct my path. My will just overrode His warnings! Before my first breath, God's purpose for my life was established, but it was not my preference. I exercised my freewill and chose an alternate route. In my youth, I did not have a clear understanding of God being sovereign. However, I began to realize it as an adult. I knew God was loving and all knowing. I understood that He only wanted the best for my life, and still, I rebelled against what I knew. God could have stopped me from making many poor choices in my life, but He will never force anyone to accept His way. Choosing God's way must be an individual's personal choice. Dismissing His way, however, results in rebellion. Beloved, rebellion always has a hidden price tag and regret is often in the small print somewhere on the label.

Rebellion means to go against authority or resist the established government. In Isaiah 46:9-10 (New Living Translation Bible) God, authoritatively states His claim as the established government over the world He created when He says, *Remember the things I have done in the past. For I alone am God! I am God, and there is none like me. Only I can tell you the future before it even happens. Everything I plan will come to pass, for I do whatever I wish.*

God is Divine Providence. He is the Creator of Heaven, Earth, and everything in it, including you and me. All things take place under His guidance and control. Even when terrible things happen, God can still redirect outcomes or bring forth results no human mind could ever conceive because the world, as out of control as it may appear, is never out of God's control. Therefore, going against His plan or purpose is a walk of rebellion. Rebellion is so easy to get into, but the consequences are so hard to get out of. Beloved, there will be consequences.

In life, many temptations compete for our attention. Without strong determination, we are bound to fall for the irresistible lure of pleasure. Sometimes, our minds will convince us that there cannot be anything wrong with indulging in something so tantalizing. At that thought, many of us have tossed aside wisdom like a troublesome neck scarf, given into reckless abandon, and embraced the forbidden thing. Warning! Once hypnotized by thoughts of gratification, we often fail to recognize unseen dangers ahead. We do not see the enemy of our destiny standing behind the scenes with the baton in hand, conducting seduction like a symphony orchestra. Once we bow to his bait and dance to his music, the devil takes the role as the spiritual authority in our lives and assumes the right to call the shots. Without even realizing it, our actions chose the enemy of God as our preferred leader. Agreeing with agents of Hell indicates that you have resisted the established government of Heaven!

Beloved, please understand. The devil will use your disobedience as his opportunity to forge a covenant with you. The danger of the contract is in the small print! That is where the disclaimer is written. The disclaimer explains that once you downplay the act of disobedience by dismissing the seriousness of it, or try to justify the behavior, the contract is automatically enforced. Then the enemy has a legal right to take the next step and bind you to the terms and consequences of a rebellious state. Ezekiel 12:2 (King James Version) says, "*Son of Man, you dwell in the midst of a rebellious house. They have eyes to see but can't. They have ears to hear but don't because they are a rebellious house.*" Rebellion makes way for demonic forces to blind your spiritual sight causing your discernment (ability to recognize, detect or identify) to malfunction! It rolls out the red carpet for demons to walk in and close your ears making it difficult for you to hear God when He speaks and clutter your mind so you are unable to comprehend the truth of what is being spoken. Before long, you will feel disconnected from God, family, and good friends. You will isolate from anyone assigned to hold you accountable. You will shut your ears to wisdom and instruction. Without intervention, your destiny will die because rebellion derails lives! Let me share this biblical example.

1 Samuel 15:23 (New Living Translation Bible), states *Rebellion is as sinful as witchcraft, and stubbornness as bad as worshiping idols. So, because you have rejected the command of the Lord, He has rejected you as king.* In this chapter of the bible, God had given a command to the King of Israel, Saul. God instructed Saul to destroy everything that was a part of the Amalekite nation including the animals. God, who is all knowing, understood what Saul did not! God knew that the Amalekites were a threat to the promises of God's people. He wanted Saul to eliminate what had the potential to destroy their future. When God determines it is no longer beneficial to keep someone or something in our lives, He is

looking out for our destiny! However, when we question God's reasoning behind a matter, we often dismiss what He says about it. Beloved, let us not be like Saul. He erred in judgement. He disobeyed the command of God and chose to spare what was appealing to him and his soldiers. Just like most unsuspecting people, Saul may have thought his decision was no big deal because he did not ponder the consequences beforehand. When the Prophet Samuel confronted him, Saul tried to justify his actions. Saul wanted Samuel to believe that his intentions for insubordination were good since he planned to sacrifice the animals to Samuel's God. Saul wanted Samuel to cosign what he had done. However, God expressed his displeasure when He informed the Prophet Samuel, that he regretted making Saul a king. Saul's consequence for disregarding what God commanded was greater than the loss of his reign as king. His defiance opened the door for an evil, angry, tormenting spirit to enter his life. When the Prophet Samuel died, Saul was left with no one to give him divine answers or guide him through life. Without the ability to hear God for himself, Saul grew frantic and sought the help of a witch. He wanted her to summon the spirit of deceased Samuel. Disobedience had taken Saul to such a low place until he turned to the grave for help. From the moment of Saul's rebellion, his life became plagued with anger, bitterness, regret, and depression which drove him to witchcraft and finally, death. Rebellion had provided an entrance to demonic influence in the life of Saul and does the same for all rebels if it is left undealt with.

Beloved, I believe that you are reading this book by divine intervention. Perhaps you realized how you have failed to conform to God's plan for your life and desire to get back on course. Possibly, you rebelled unintentionally or ignorantly because you could not see behind the mask of what approached you. Had you seen what the implications would be, you may have never made the choice. Yet, you are still in a struggle mentally and emotionally. God has stepped in right now to interrupt the rampage of rebellion and stop its aftermath. However, you will never end the plight of rebellion without obedience. You must pinpoint and acknowledge areas of your life where you rejected the Lord's will. Next, you must repent. Repent means to change your mind about something, feel remorse or sorrow for your action, agree that something was not right and turn away from it. Once you acknowledge your wrongdoing and embrace the remorse you may feel, you sincerely apologize to God and any other parties involved, then grab hold of a determination to do things the right way which is God's way!

Repentance for rebellion is mandatory. Once you identify an action or a thought as rebellious, you must fight to release it from your heart and mind with a determination to never entertain it again. If you justify wrong or defend wrong, you will repeat wrong. Once you sincerely acknowledge God as your Creator and Jesus Christ as your Savior, strive daily to value the gift of life He has given to you. Life is priceless! You and I could never repay God for it. The best we can do is develop a strong love and deep respect so that the idea of shortchanging Him with the breath He has blessed us with becomes deplorable. When true repentance becomes easy, rebellion becomes difficult.

You are not your own. You have been bought with a price. God loved you so much, He surrendered His only son, Jesus, to die on the cross for every defiant sin you would ever commit. God gave such a costly sacrifice as an open expression of how much He values you. Release rebellion open your heart and concede to God's will for your life. Right now, at this very moment, I come against the spirit of rebellion at work in your life, in the Name of Jesus Christ. I plead the blood of Jesus against it and bind its influence! I speak that the love of the Lord will flood your heart in an overwhelming and undeniable way. I pray that you surrender to that flow even now in Jesus' Name. I pray that as you embrace the powerful love of Jesus, you will simultaneously let go of rebellious thoughts, actions, and deeds. I command your spirit and mind to be broken from the grip of rebellion now, In Jesus' Name. I pray the spirit of obedience and discipleship will rest upon you and take a hold of your very being in Jesus' Mighty name. I call a change to your thoughts and declare that your mind is being transformed by the Power of the Holy Spirit. The Mind of Christ is rising within you. The Love of Jesus Christ is arresting your heart. Forgiveness is flooding your soul. You are being spiritually renewed! Thank You, Father. In Jesus Name! AMEN!

Redirected from rebellion!

Hear my prayer, O LORD, and give ear unto my cry. Do not be silent at my tears.... (Psalms 39:12 NKJV)

CHAPTER 4

Daddy, I'm Hurt!

I grew up down south in the most country parts with both of my parents in the home. In our household, my dad went to work, and my mom stayed home to take care of my sisters and me. Our family life was a very structured one, although we were a far cry from being middle class. Mama got up every morning and prepared a homemade breakfast. I can remember the smell of bacon frying in the kitchen. That aroma would draw me right out of bed. We sat as a family and ate breakfast together every morning. We never ate without giving God thanks for our meals.

My sister and I had responsibilities growing up. We gathered eggs from the hen house in the mornings and watered the pigs every evening. We sometimes had to help gather wood for the wood burning heater. We washed clothes in our rolling pin washing machine and hung them on the clothesline to dry. We grew most of our food. My parents were immensely proud of their vegetable gardens. My sister and I often helped pull weeds, pick beans and squash, gather tomatoes, cut okra, and dug up potatoes, but the real reward for me was always watermelon! I can recall sweltering summer days of lying on my back in the grass lost in the blue of beautiful skies. Life seemed so right to me during those times until one day! Beloved, life can change in 24 hours! I will never forget that day when my mom needed to take my grandma to town. My sister and I ended up staying with my uncle. We were about 4 and 5 years old. He was maybe 19 or 20 years old. My sister and I were playing outside when my uncle came and stood in the door and watched us play for a while. Then he said it was time for us to take a nap. My sister asked for more time to play. I said nothing, but I felt an uneasiness. I did not understand it then, but my stomach felt like it tied up into knots. My eyes stung from the tears that threatened to fall. Fear gripped my heart. I can remember feeling like something was wrong and I wanted to run, but I did not. We went into the house. It seemed so dark and dreary. We followed him down the long hallway. I can still remember the chilling screech of the door as he pushed it open and told us to lie down on the bed. He put me in the middle beside him and my sister against the wall. We laid there in strict silence for a while, but I could not dare go to sleep. My sister finally drifted off. My heart pounded when I noticed that he turned to look at me. There was something disturbing about his eyes. I had never seen that look before. It was not simply different, it was devious. Suddenly his hands were inside my short pants and he was fondling me. I tried to pull his hands out, but he was too strong for me. Without warning, he was on top of me with the seat of my pants pulled to one side. I could not breathe because his chest was against my face. I struggled against his weight to get free but failed. Suddenly,

I felt something hard pushed into me. The pain of it forced a piercing scream from the deepest part of me. I began to cry. My sister woke up and started fighting him. I remember her words as she struggled and cried. "Don't do that to my sister. Do it to me if you have to, just don't do that to her!" Immediately, he turned to get on top of her and we both started to fight him. I do not remember much after that. The moments that passed were blurred with confusion and disbelief. The sound of mama's tires turning in from the highway caused my heart to pound harder. I did not know what would happen next. He jumped up and made us leave his room as he threatened that we had better not tell or we would be sorry. I tried to hurry down the hall, but my legs would not go together. Walking was painful. I never felt like that before. I moved slowly towards the car. With each wide legged step, fear filled my heart and forced tears from my eyes. I thought maybe mama would sense that something was wrong. But I dared not to speak one word while we were still in that yard. I wanted to say 'Mama, Uncle Mel did something bad to me' but his threat choked the words right out of me. When we got home, mama was unlocking the door when I mustered enough courage to barely whisper, 'Mama, something is wrong down there. I can't close my legs!' I wanted her to ask me why, but she said nothing! I was baffled by her silence. My young mind tried to comprehend it. Did she know? Did she hear me? Or did she ignore me? Either way, I was too ashamed and scared to repeat it. We went inside. I felt dazed and numb. I think I was in a state of shock. I recall that mama ran a tub of water for me. When she left the bathroom, I sat there and cried. Mama was always good to my sister and me. She was one of the sweetest women I knew. I was glad she was my mom. She was strong! She held our home together! I wanted her to know what happened to me. I longed for her to get mad or cry or hug me. I know she would have done all those things and probably fight too if I were brave enough to say it, but I was not. I just sat in the tub battling the details of what had occurred along with so many other thoughts. I wondered what I had done wrong. I wanted to call mama back into the bathroom to get some answers, but I did not. I chose to avoid what I did not know how to confront.

Later in the day, I was lying across my bed looking out of my window. I knew daddy would be home soon. He pulled up and went to the wood yard to cut wood for us. I slipped on my shoes and ran outside to meet him. The closer I got to Daddy, the more the tears fought to escape my eyes. I tried to hold them in, but I lost the battle. Daddy asked me what was wrong as he took a knee and reached for me with open arms. I blurted between the sobs, 'Uncle Mel hurt me down there, Daddy'.

"What the Hell!" He shouted. Then suddenly, he composed himself, hugged me and said, "Baby, don't worry. Daddy will take care of it for you! Go inside and lay down and don't worry 'bout a thing. Daddy got it!"

As I went back into the house, I dried my tears. I knew Daddy was going to fix it. I had faith in my daddy! From my bedroom window, I saw Daddy's red pickup truck tearing down the dirt road leaving clouds of dust behind it. In a few minutes, I saw him headed back towards home and noticed that my Uncle Mel was in the truck with him. Daddy took Uncle Mel behind that woodshed and beat him bloody. Then the next news circulating was how Uncle Mel suddenly decided to leave town. No one ever spoke of that day again.

I thought that Daddy would fix everything. Truth is, Daddy did what he knew to do to fix the situation, but Daddy could not fix me. The fear, betrayal, distrust, disgust, and regret that grabbed me that day tried to maintain its hold throughout my life. In my uncle's room, I lost a part of me greater than my virginity. I lost my confidence! The void filled quickly with shame. I walked into that room as an innocent child. I came out shattered, scarred and burdened with a secret. I kept replaying the moment. What if I had done something differently? I sensed something was wrong. Why did I not run away? Why was I so quick to give up the fight for myself, but I fought for my sister? Those questions continued to haunt me into my adulthood.

I came to realize that Satan loves to execute vicious attacks against potentially powerful leaders while they are young and mentally immature. The Holy Bible gives Moses in Exodus chapters 1 and 2 as well as Jesus in Matthew chapter 2 as examples. Both Moses and Jesus were destined to become powerful leaders of deliverance. However, they were both born during times when the government had issued decrees to destroy all males under the age of 2 years old. I am convinced that such demonic decrees are still being released against the children of destiny today. Some of you have been the victim of such satanic assaults while you were young. Others of you can see the evidence of these attacks in the lives of your own children or children that you are close to. When a person's future intimidates the enemy, he makes that individual his target and sets out to destroy them.

I was a victim of childhood rape because I was a child of destiny from birth. Satan's strategy was released against my life to stop my development and it did not matter who he bewitched to use as a pawn in his game. Unfortunately, my uncle was available. Physically, he snatched my virginity. Psychologically, he seized my royalty. Satan used my uncle to rip away my princess dress and toss it with my tiara! I spent years of my life trying to reconnect with my inner princess before I could discover my inner queen!

Unforgiveness is a dangerous game. The enemy wanted my life to stay hemmed up in it so all the blessings God wanted to give me would be held up as well. I realized that forgiveness was going to be the bridge that brought me over into a better place, but crossing it was not going to be easy.

Rape broke me. For years, the aftermath tried to dominate my life. As much as I imagined confronting what was troubling me, I feared the outcome of doing so. I was terrified of how I would react, so I used that as an excuse to do nothing. I learned that inaction can still bring forth reaction whether you confront a situation or not. Although I refused to approach the matter, I still acted out in ways I would not ordinarily behave. I experienced anxiety attacks, trust issues, hostility, crying spells, bouts of depression and outbursts of anger. Although I tried to hide it, I discovered that suppressed anger is still anger and volatile under the right conditions! Concealed bitterness is still bitterness and subject to seek revenge.

Although I was raped as a little girl, I found myself walking around as a young lady harboring a heated hatred for my uncle. In my thoughts, If I never saw him again, that would still be too soon. However, being out of sight did not make him out of mind. One day, when I was about 22 years old, He came back home. When I first heard the news, extreme dread paralyzed me! When I finally saw him, a volcano of fury erupted in my soul! Before long, he had a new wife of whom I did not think he deserved. I wanted him alone and miserable for the rest of his pathetic life! Every time he saw me, he acted as if nothing had ever happened and I thought of the many ways he could die. We were both working in the same town, about 20 miles from home. He would be waiting at the highway every day trying to hitch a ride to work. I would look his way so that he knew I saw him and then pass by. I played that vindictive game until the day the Holy Spirit spoke to my heart. I knew I could not keep living that way. I did not want to live a life that was hell bound because of a grudgeful spirit. So, driving home from work one evening, I had a talk with the Lord. I first thanked Him that his mercy and grace kept me the day I was raped. It could have been worse. The spirit of rape could have been accompanied by a spirit of murder. My uncle could have killed my sister and I and ran! I thanked God for Mama and Grandma showing up when they did. Then, the greatest confession I could have ever made spilled from my heart. 'Daddy, I'm hurt!' Oh my God, how I cried uncontrollably upon the release of those words! What felt like a thousand tears later, I asked God to heal my heart and forgive me for hating my uncle. I prayed for strength and courage to do what I needed to do the next morning. The next day came, and God granted me courage. I did not pass him. I stopped and picked him up. The conversation was general and pretty one sided at first with him doing all the talking. I did not speak much, because I was gathering the strength to say what I needed to say. About 5 minutes from his job, I blurted it out. 'Why did you rape me? I was a child! Why did you do that to me?' I asked. He sat quietly for a few seconds and then he denied it. "I never did that to you, Sherry. You must have dreamed that" he said nervously.

Those words of denial provoked a strong desire to knock his head off! Restrained instead by the Holy Spirit, I said 'Oh yes you did! I remember! I will never forget. You were wrong and I hated you for a long, long time. Now you are back here and riding in my car! You were dirty and nasty, and you never said you were sorry, but you know what? I forgive you. I am not doing it for you. I am doing it for me. I will never be free from this if I don't forgive you'. As the words left my lips, I struggled internally to rationalize what was being said.

When I finished speaking, we were at his job sight. He said, "I'm sorry," and got out of the car. I pulled away and drove onto my job. I sobbed, but this cry was different. It was a cry of relief. I was finally letting go of the hurt, bitterness and unforgiveness I had been carrying for about 17 years. I did not realize how heavy it was until the weight of it began to lift from me. As much as I felt justified to be angry and hate my uncle, Holy Spirit helped me to understand my choice to remain that way was keeping me in a personal prison. Not only was I giving my uncle the power of control over my life, I was granting the demon of rape permission to incarcerate my future. My decision to forgive was necessary for my release. I discovered liberty could be my choice, but not my reality until I was willing to let go of the reason I was imprisoned! I had to surrender my right to be angry. The enemy did not want me to confront the matter because my liberty was bound by my silence. When I broke the silence, I broke the bands that held me hostage all those years.

I learned from experience that our minds are powerful. Not only can we make ourselves believe that we are over hurts, betrayals, and disappointments, we can convince others also. It seems more socially acceptable to lie about how you truly feel than it is to tell the truth sometimes. Therefore, many people live everyday publicly pretending to be happy while secretly settling for mediocrity and misery. Sadly, I have done it myself. I can clearly remember the times in my life where I walked around functioning in dysfunction, with a façade that nothing bothered me. That image was so far from the truth. I was not over stuff. I just learned to live like I was. Many challenges came to crush me but with each one, I somehow mustered the strength to keep moving, healed or not. Although I mastered the art of *rolling with the punches*, I discovered that was not always mentally or emotionally healthy.

I am sure you can recall a turn of events which may have thrown your life into an upheaval. Some of you are still hearing the harsh words spoken at you. Even today, they continue to bring tears to your eyes and cause pain to linger in your heart. Others are still suffering from the agony of the daggers of betrayal in your back and chest. Someone reading this is living in regret over a decision that persistently gives you nightmares. Somebody's peace has been plundered by paranoia because you fear being found out. Some reader has a childhood secret so painful; they still cannot bear to talk about it. Sometimes, situations are too devastating to revisit. Once buried, many consider it best to leave the matter covered than to deal with the embarrassment of excavating again. However, buried things tend to resurface sometimes. You see, anything that remains undealt with in your life is an area of weakness prone to breaking. You are only as strong as your weakest point. Beloved, God wants your life whole. He wants you healed once and for all from everything that caused you emotional trauma. Adopt this truth in your heart. It is no longer acceptable to seal the memories of painful events, words, or actions away in the recesses of your mind and label them, "DO NOT OPEN!" God will grace you to face it. But He needs your confession. Even if you must force the words from your lips, tell Him, "Daddy, I'm hurt!"

How often do we run to other sources for help and save God as a last resort? Beloved, it is time to run to God. I thought my natural daddy could fix everything, including me, but I found myself disappointed. Some of you may have sought out other alternatives to get you through or beyond your own personal ordeal. You may have placed your expectation upon a spouse, friend, parent, pastor or maybe even a psychic, believing they could help you only to end up downhearted when they failed. Let me encourage you. God has an abundant life prepared for you. The plan has already been made and carefully laid out before you, but you have got to go to Him. The reality is, no other option will work to fully resolve your situation. I understand that maybe you received some temporary consolation, but Jesus has the everlasting solution. He can reach into the deepest parts of your heart and soul to make things new again. Give Him all the pain, embarrassment, hurt, anger, disgust, and disappointment. Relinquish to Him all your pieces. Regardless of how big or small, God wants to handle it for you. He is your Father if you have asked Him to be. If you have not, it is a perfect time right now. He is concerned about you. He loves you. You can trust Him to handle whatever burdens you. He not only knows how to fix any situation, but He knows how to restore where you have been broken. In Psalms 31 King David found himself needing the help of the Lord in a situation that wanted to overpower him. King David cried out to God for help declaring that his trust was in the Lord. In verse 8 of that chapter, David rejoiced when he said God had not given him into the hands of his enemy but instead, set his feet in a spacious place. God wants to do the same thing for you. You have been confined to a small area long enough. No longer allow the bars of your past struggles to incarcerate you. It is time to make the confession that has the power to unlock your prison cell. God wants you free to run and skip through the meadows of life! By His Almighty Power, He wants to bring you out of what has vowed to overpower you. He wants to set you in a greater place. He said, "I will never leave you nor forsake you". That promise is recorded several times in the Bible. You may feel like the biggest failure, but you are not. Your situation may tell you that God abandoned you or that He does not want anything to do with you, but truthfully, He has always been your bodyguard! You did not die in anything that had an assignment to destroy you. You are still here purposefully reading this book. *Lamentations 3:22-23 says It is of the Lord's mercies that we are not consumed. His compassions fail not. They are new every morning. Great is His faithfulness.* It has been the Lord's unfailing mercy and compassion that ushered you through every life shattering situation you have encountered. I want you to realize that God has been a Constant in your life. When others changed on you, He never did. He has been a very present help in your times of trouble. Rather you acknowledged His Presence, or you disregarded it, God was there like a strong dependable father would be. Even through situations where you possibly blamed Him because you did not understand the reasoning behind the matter, God did not leave you. Maybe you have been so strong all your life trying to hold everything and everybody else together, neglecting yourself in the process. Do something for you! Today, make up in your mind to go to God and have a conversation that can change your life forever. Put it all on the table. You do not have to censor your words with Him. You can let down your walls and trust Him with your vulnerabilities. As with any difficult, yet necessary conversation, you may not know where to start. May I suggest that you start with three little words? They worked for me. "Daddy, I'm hurt".

Redirected from the pain that never wanted to let go!

Daddy is Here

I read the tears of my daughter's eyes. I heard the words of her silent cries.

I felt the pain of her broken heart and cringed from the sting of the fiery darts.

Challenges came to destroy her will and leave her with promises unfulfilled.

If only my daughter would run to me. There is comfort in my arms and safety at my feet.

Oh, Precious Jewel. Please draw near.

Hear me whisper, "Daddy is here".

Yes, I am her Father. I will intervene.

For her, I will create miracles the world has never seen.

I will rise and declare her life is not done.

This is just an intermission. Her best is yet to come.

Naysayers, Haters, Spectators and Perpetrators,

Please keep your seats!

I need you as witnesses when she rises from defeat!

You see, that is my daughter. She wears my name! I am her Protector. I will heal her pain!

Daughter, you will get up from this. Power will be yours. I will be your help. You can rest assured.

I will adorn you with lace and sprinkle you with grace. They will see my glory radiate from your face. I will hold you through this until the challenge is no more. Then I will show you greater things that I have in store. No matter how hard it gets. Have no fear. I am reaching for you. Your Daddy is Here.

From the Heart of the Lord

-Cheryl W. Beaufort

"May your choices reflect your hopes not your fears."

-Nelson Mandela

CHAPTER 5

MY CHOICE BETRAYED ME

When I was young, I remember watching a game show called Let's Make A Deal hosted by a man named Monty Hall. The people in the audience would masquerade themselves in strange costumes like dairy maids, animals and even hotdogs. They wanted to stand out in the crowd to increase their chances of being selected by the host. There would be three doors on stage. Ultimately, if the chosen contestant met some request of the host, he or she would be given the chance to select a door. Each of the three doors had a prize. Of course, every contestant desired the grand prize because it was always valuable. But with each choice, there was the possibility of getting “zonked”. A zonk was a worthless prize that nobody wanted. When the wrong door was chosen, disappointment and regret was evident upon the player’s face.

Thinking back, I realize this game show portrays the lives of many people, including myself. How often have we found ourselves waiting to be chosen by someone we thought would make us winners? How often have we dressed out of character to increase our chances of being selected by someone only drawn to the image of who we portrayed ourselves to be? There is nothing wrong with a desire to be chosen. I believe it is woven into the core of who we are. The downside of that desire is a demon called Desperation! Merriam Webster Dictionary defines desperation as a state of hopelessness that leads to rashness. In other words, we can covet something so strongly but the fear of never having it can cause us to do some crazy things to get it. This is especially true in love and relationships! Sometimes, society will make a person feel as though they are less than if they are not in a relationship or marriage. If we succumb to that pressure, we can find ourselves living out the role of someone else's fantasy or one that we created just to be chosen. In my own life, I have shamefully compromised my values and morals, dummied down my strengths, and conformed to the mindset of another who did not know how to honor me. Let me make this statement loud and clear. NOBODY IS GOING TO HONOR YOU WHEN YOU DO NOT HONOR YOURSELF! Truthfully, I could not expect honor from another when I displayed behaviors that brought dishonor upon myself. My actions showed that I did not honor who God told me I was. How could I stay angry at someone who followed my lead? After all, I showed evidence of a desperate woman. Like the game show, Let's Make a Deal, I got caught up by the opinions of the crowd around me. The hype of other people's relationship rattled my emotions, panic struck, and I made the wrong decision! My choice betrayed me! I want to share a biblical story with you of a woman in the bible who fell victim to this same mindset.

In biblical times, culture placed a lot of pressure on a woman to be married and have children. Her status in society was measured in large by those two conditions. No husband, no children, no respect! Genesis 38:6-24 depicts a portion of the life of a woman named Tamar. According to the customs of that time, women were considered property and were not allowed to choose a spouse for themselves. Tamar was chosen to be the wife of a young man named Er. While the two were married, Er committed some undisclosed act which displeased God, so he was killed before he could get his wife pregnant. After the death of her husband, Tamar had to conform to the set of circumstances that was placed upon her. Custom mandated that she would be passed on to the next surviving brother so she could birth a child which would continue the family blood line. Because a barren woman was a symbol of shame in those times, Tamar's burden to conceive and birth a child was great. However, she was passed to a brother named Onan who could care less about her needs or her heart. Onan gratified himself at the expense of her purpose. He had sex with her then wasted his sperm on the ground instead of impregnating her. Tamar found herself used and dismissed. You may be able to identify with Tamar at this point. You understand what it is like to be neglected by someone who did not acknowledge your value neither were they capable of appraising the pricelessness of your purpose. Understand this, Beloved! God is not sleep!

Onan died because he displeased the Lord. It is possible that his death was a part of his penalty for sabotaging what Tamar was ordained to do. Still feeling the stress to fulfill purpose but not seeing the means to do so, Tamar was left wondering what was next for her. The father-in- law, Judah, advised Tamar that she should return to her father's house until Judah's baby boy was old enough to marry. At which time, He vowed to bring Tamar back so she could continue the family's blood line by conceiving from Judah's youngest son. Tamar made the choice to trust Judah. However, Judah secretly blamed Tamar for the death of his two sons. So, he sent her away, clothed in widow's garments, carrying an empty promise that he never intended to keep. Tamar's choice betrayed her. The Bible says some time had passed, but Tamar finally realized an unsettling truth. Judah had reneged on his oath to her.

There would be no baby for her to swaddle or hold close to her breast. It seemed her hopes were swallowed up in Judah's lie!

In my life, I have seen people handle deception and betrayal differently. Some sufferers lose their fight and refuse to get up and embrace life again. They submit to the circumstances and settle for the hand dealt. Their lives become overrun with negative thinking, so they seldom expect anything good to happen. A lack of trust allows suspicion to rule. Discouragement clouds any possibility of a better life. Pessimism governs their conversation and destroys their ambition. On the other hand, some victims of betrayal develop a fierce determination to make something happen by any means necessary. Once raging, that fire can only be quenched by results.

Tamar had been lied to, disappointed, abandoned, used, shamed, and discarded like a piece of trash. Allow me to imagine. Over the course of time, she wrestled with the spirit of rejection. As she rested upon her bed at night, her eyelids searched for sleep among the darkness but gave way to tears of hurt and anger instead. Bitterness turned into revenge as she paced the floor in deep thought. Then one day, she was struck by an epiphany. Her widow's garments were not just a symbol of mourning, they were symbolic of separation. The relationships had ended but her purpose still had a pulse. Death came to disconnect her from every negative thing she had experienced. Nevertheless, the mandate of what she felt destined to do would not die! Opportunity presented itself, and she seized it. Desperate for results, Tamar came out of her widow's garments and disguised herself as a harlot. Before long, she was wrapped in a robe of seduction held loosely together by a belt of manipulation! Her plot to get Judah to come into her was initiated by the spirit of revenge which entered her first. Vindictiveness were the carefully placed rose petals which lured Judah's feet. With thoughtless anticipation, the unsuspecting father in law joined his veiled daughter in law upon the bed of deception. But not before Tamar collected surety from Judah to make certain he kept his word to her that time. Tamar ended up pregnant with twins of which, Judah was the father. As the news of her pregnancy began to travel, it reached

Judah's ears. Someone informed him that his daughter in law had played the prostitute. The report fueled his urge for vengeance. Judah sought to destroy Tamar. He had not yet discovered that Tamar was the prostitute he had shared a one-night stand with after his wife died. To end Judah's witch hunt, Tamar had what she held as collateral delivered to him. She sent an announcement as well. If Judah could identify the possessions, he would know who the father of her children was. I can only envision the shocking guilt Judah must have felt upon recognizing his personal belongings and his wrongdoing. Tamar did not allow herself to be betrayed by him again. Her choice may not have been a socially accepted one, but she made it based upon what she wanted for her future. She did not allow fear of other people's opinion to stop her! She was willing to accept the consequences of her decisions. Tamar risked it all but ended up with the grand prize! She gave birth to twins and continued Judah's bloodline. Her mission was accomplished!

Let us look deeper, Beloved. Tamar transformed from a mourning widow and took on the behavior of a provocative harlot! Why did she change personalities like that? It was her response to being betrayed!

Beloved, please know that you can be on the greatest flight of your life and get slammed by a situation capable of creating a horrific crash! No matter how strong you believe you are, recovery can be difficult, especially when you realize that your choice created the turbulence. If you ever reach the danger zone where your mood or behavior can change faster than you can flip a switch, that is an indication that it is time to stop and get a good grip! Locate the power source of what is controlling you and disconnect it quickly! Otherwise, what is left unresolved can manifest through multiple personality changes that will keep your life looking like one gigantic roller coaster of emotions.

The only way to guard against our choices ending in betrayal is to get help when choosing. Proverbs 3:5 Good News Translation says *trust in the Lord with all your heart. Never rely on what you think you know. Remember the Lord in everything you do, and He will show you the right way.* This is such an important yet overlooked key to life, Beloved. We do not always take the time to find out from the Lord which door would be the right door or which choice would be the best one. It is almost inconceivable that God would trust us with the sole right to make any decision we prefer for our lives even though we are His created beings. Yet, God gave the gift of freewill to everyone. It is an immensely powerful gift, but without supervision, it can be a very destructive one. I find it amazing how many times we can make decisions, devoid of God's counsel, which end in disaster. Although, God will not force His choice on us, He is in favor of consultations. I believe He desires that we love, trust and reverence Him enough to seek His will for our lives and move accordingly. Job 12:13 New International Version says *To God belong wisdom and power; counsel and understanding are His.*

Jeremiah 29:11 is one of my favorite scriptures. The New Living Translation says, "*For I know the plans I have for you,*" *says the Lord.* "*They are plans for good and not for disaster, to give you a future and a hope.*" When we come into agreement with God's plan for our lives and submit fully, we become like chess pieces. We get moved by the power of His hand and will. When we allow God to play us without resistance, we will witness His plan unfold before our eyes. God will move us right into victory. The bible gives confirmation. God spoke these words in Isaiah 46:10 (King James Version) " *Declaring the end from the beginning, and from ancient times the things that are not yet done, saying, My counsel shall stand, and I will do all my pleasure.*" This scripture indicates that God had power to declare everything that would happen in the future because He had already determined outcomes before the events came to pass. His counsel brought forth results. God clearly stated that *His counsel would prevail and bring forth His good pleasure.* God has a plan to help us live a life of victory, but this is impossible without consulting with Him before we make decisions. Although it makes good sense to seek God's wisdom and counsel, we do not always exercise that good sense, do we? Sometimes, it is because we do not know how.

There is not a set formula for knowing the will of God for your life. It comes through building a relationship with Him through His son, Jesus. In life, we build relationships with others through conversations and by spending time together. We should follow the same protocol when getting to know Jesus. We cannot talk to Him through the phone, but we should seek conversation daily through prayer. We cannot read what He has to say through text messages. But we can learn His heart through the text of the bible. The more we learn and accept Him, the more we grow in Him. The closer we get to Jesus, the more He will reveal His choices for our lives. We may hear a quiet voice inside of our hearts telling us what to do. We may feel an urge to move in a certain direction. We may just have an unexplainable knowledge that we should or should not do a thing. The stronger our relationship grows with Him, the more we will obey Him. As our obedience increases, wrong decisions decrease. Let us pray.

Father God, we come to you now in the name of Your Son and our Savior, Jesus Christ. We acknowledge and repent to You for any action or thought that went against Your will and nature. Please forgive us for our wrong. We ask humbly that You will bless each of us with your grace and mercy. We ask that You heal us from the damage of our poor decisions. In the name of Jesus, we break the stagnation of disappointments! We decree accelerated forward movement now in Jesus Name.

We plead the blood of Jesus over our lives. We plead the blood of Jesus against every spirit of shame, regret, brokenness, or revenge. We openly confess those things to you now. We renounce them along with any hidden feeling or thought that does not please you, Lord. We pray that the power be broken from these things and from any other thing causing instability in our lives now in Jesus' Name. We pray the spirit of liberty break and eliminate the spirit of bondage at work in our lives right now, in the name of Jesus Christ. We pray peace, wisdom and obedience overtake us. We pray the spirit of healing and restoration will rest upon us now in Jesus' Name. We pray that we will seek Your heart and Your will for our lives like never before. We pray, according to Jeremiah 29:11, that

Your plan for a great future be executed in our lives and prosperity finds us in mind blowing ways. We ask all these petitions in the mighty name of our Savior, Jesus Christ. We believe by faith that we have all we have asked. We receive it with thankful hearts! In Jesus Name. Amen!

Redirected from the torment of wrong choices!

Call to Me, and I will answer you, and show you great and mighty things, which you do not know. (Jeremiah 33:3 NKJV)

CHAPTER 6

A WAKE-UP CALL: YOU DON'T GO THROUGH JUST FOR YOU

The silence of the night was interrupted by a screaming drill sergeant. The sudden outburst of my alarm clock grew louder the more I tried to ignore it. Each beep poked at me insisting that I leave my nest of warmth and comfort. I finally gave in. As I sat on the side of my bed, trying to make sense of day and time, I rubbed away the blur from my eyes thinking, "Really? Is it six o'clock already?" My feet shuffled around beneath me, trying to find my slippers that seem to be playing a game of hide and seek. I dragged across the carpet and made my way towards the annoying buzzer. My toe met the dresser first. "Ouch! What a rude way to say good morning!" I thought as I groped around until I found the magical alarm off button which caused a hush to fall again in the dimly lit room. I began to pray quietly as I headed to the bathroom for a wake-up shower, "Father, I really need you today". No sooner than the clouds of white lather would wrap my body, misty sprinkles rinsed them away. Suddenly, a vision appeared before me. I saw a large group of women huddled together in the shape of a triangle. They all seemed to be looking up at me as I watched them from an elevated place. However, I could not identify their faces. As I peered into the shadows of the dimly lit area, the distance from which I watched made it impossible to distinguish who was there. Each face seemed veiled. As I moved in closer, one of the faces came into focus and I realized that she was me! Upon that revelation, the vision faded leaving behind a heavy burden. Suddenly, I felt the powerful urge to pray.

"Father, thank you for allowing me to feel your presence this morning. Holy Spirit, I need you. I feel lost! I do not know what I am supposed to do at this point. Please give me clarity. Father, make your will known to me." I pleaded.

Billows of hurt rose inside of me. My tears joined the flowing water at my feet. It was as if my inner heart continued to cry out to God even though my mouth had given up the fight. Suddenly, I was overwhelmed by an unexplainable knowledge. Just like that, my mind shifted from confusion to clarity. I was experiencing another one of those moments again. The moment when I just know without explanation of how. I continued to pray, "Father, Help me! I feel the agony of wounded souls. These women have been abused and left with rejection and pain. They have been mishandled by negligent people. Some daggers were plunged deep into their hearts by the hands of those who were given access. I am overwhelmed by the silent cries of their hearts. But how can I help them when I am one of them? Oh God, please!! I cannot stay here!

There is another level I must reach to help this group of women! Get me pass this stuck place so I can guide others."

In an early morning shower, I had experienced the power of God in such a tangible, mind blowing way. Something pass my natural comprehension was awakened in that moment! There was no preacher, no music, no one leading me into worship. It was just me and God. I then understood that God would meet you wherever He could get your attention. Especially when you are the type who tries to avoid destiny! You see, I loved God, but I ignorantly limited His pull on my life! At times, I could feel the pull of His Presence become so intense. Purposely, I would shift my focus to something different. It was like sending Him the message that I was not ready yet. I knew deep inside that The Lord Jesus wanted to use my life for something more than what I was doing, but I feared. I doubted that God really could use me past where I was. So, I kept that part of my life under the anesthesia of preoccupation! I kept doing what I wanted to do until *my will* and *His Way* collided! *My will* was to stay tucked away in some mental corner of oblivion pretending that my life was fine just the way it was. After all, things were not that bad. Why complicate matters? The problem was, God did not agree with me! God had to make me aware that He would not allow me to stay paralyzed by my passivity nor continue to prolong other people's process through my pretending! People were waiting on me to be delivered so I could help them break free!

This word is for someone other than me! You can expect this spiritual head on collision to happen to you too! There will come a time when what you want for your life and what God has said about your life will clash! Let me share this very truth. You can wrestle against God for as long as you have strength! You will not win! Not in this battle, Beloved! He has released a Word over your life before you ever entered it. His Word cannot return to Him without yielding results! I heard the spirit of the Lord say that some of you are spiritually late and pregnant! Pretending that the baby is not there does not erase the fact that the pregnancy is real! You are bearing people's word of deliverance in your belly. You possess the key to unlock their doors. You hold the battering ram for their breakthrough! Hear me, Beloved! What another person desperately needs is in you! You embody their answer! God wants to use you! Yes you, flaws and all.

I have learned that some of the best treasure is hidden among what others would consider trash! People often look at the current struggle of others and make assumptions about their outcome. A person may be down for a moment, but that does not mean he or she will not rise later! My own life taught me not to judge an individual's "*now*" because I can't see his or her "*after this*". I have met many people who have been drug dealers, drug addicts, alcoholics, prostitutes, and homosexuals. I glorify God for these redeemed individuals who surrendered their lives to Christ Jesus. These overcomers remain examples of how Jesus can reconstruct the broken and restore all things lost. I salute them for being soldiers who survived! Such individuals had to build their testimonies under extremely challenging circumstances. Everybody did not make it out alive. There were some casualties of war. Nevertheless, those who lived to tell can lead others to the hill of liberty.

Maybe you feel like your life has been such a series of disappointments. You just do not want to try again or run the risk of letting down anyone else…not even yourself. Maybe some ordeals left you feeling like damaged goods with nothing to offer. Beloved, please hear this. Somebody needs your story to relate to. They need your words of triumph to lift them from the slums of poor decisions. Realize that it took everything you ever experienced in your life to prepare you for your Kingdom assignment. Your adversity authorized you. God trusted you with the trouble so you would be equipped to aid someone else in their transformation. BEEP! BEEP! BEEP! Beloved, do you hear that buzzer going off in your spirit? It is your wake-up call! Get up dear! Rise and shine from your slumbering places. You did not go through for just you! Your audience awaits. You have work to do.

Redirected from slumber when purpose is calling!

He has given me a new song to sing, a hymn of praise to our God. Many will see what He has done and be amazed. They will put their trust in the LORD.(Psalms 40:3 NLT)

CHAPTER 7

STARTING OVER

WHEN GOD SWITCHES YOUR SONG!

I have always loved music. I do not limit myself to any specific genre. I like what I like. I have discovered that some songs easily communicate what I find difficult to articulate. I have been motivated by the right melody when nothing else could inspire me. On many restless nights, I was calmed by the hushed harmony of the perfect lullaby as I drifted off to sleep. Music can create moments and express moods! Metaphorically speaking, if my life were a song, what a mixed composition the listeners would hear! There would probably be the loud clashing of symbols, screeching guitars, and a melancholy organ mingled with senseless lyrics!

When I compare music and life, I find it empowering to have a choice of what I want in my atmosphere! I, like yourself, have the freedom to leave what I like to hear on repeat or silence what I find disturbing. Sometimes life can become irritating like a glitching CD. In such instances, we must determine the source of the disruption. The ruckus can stem from the need of a simple cleaning or be as severe as something damaged beyond repair. I have learned that sometimes, it is not the CD at all! There is a need for a new player!

I can recall a time when my world had grown violently turbulent. If my heart had a song, blues would have been the genre! I paced the floor of my bedroom. Tears flowed uncontrollably. I fought hard to halt them, but my feelings were stronger than my logic and the tears won. Life, as I knew it, was disintegrating in my hands. I watched the fine particles of marriage, family, and ministry seep through my fingers. A war was raging inside of me, and it felt like I was losing. Emotions kept chiding me of how foolish I would be to tear up my own home and threatened me to stop. But truth reassured me that I had spent enough time, tears and effort trying to patch what was damaged beyond repair. Although I had become engaged in a massive struggle to let go what was familiar, I knew I had to. I finally came to understand that sentimental value is not a good enough reason to put your destiny in danger. Without even realizing it, I had settled for quick fixes for an awfully long time. Somewhere along the line, I lost hope and stopped believing for something new!

Months prior, I was overwhelmed by a need to deep clean my home. I went through every room decluttering and purging what was old, no longer needed and taking up unnecessary space. I did not know at that time that my actions were God's strategy. What I was doing naturally in my home prophesied what God was getting ready to do spiritually and emotionally in my life! When it was time for me to clean my bedroom, I started in my closet which was so symbolic. (Oh, the secrets we keep and the problems we hide in our closets!) As I sorted through some clothes, I heard the Spirit of the Lord say, "*I am getting ready to show you some things. You can handle it now."* I did not comprehend the magnitude of what was about to unfold in my life. Before long, I found myself caught in an emotional sandstorm. Most times, I could not see what was coming. I just felt the repetitive sting as truths hit and lies were exposed. Prayer was my response. I decided to take a 30-day consecration period to seek God. Although people were all around me giving their opinions of what I should do, I needed to hear God clearly. I did not want to move outside of His will for me. During that time, I prayed, fasted, and studied God's Holy Word. My front porch became my altar. I sat there day after day, early mornings, and late evenings as I listened to the birds serenade me with their songs of worship. God's presence never failed to show up and sit with me. I had indescribable encounters filled with moments of revelation, healing, and breakthrough. As I sat in the counsel of the Holy Spirit. I grew more sensitive to the voice and Presence of God. My spiritual comprehension became so sharp, it was almost intimidating.

One day, about halfway through my consecration period, I was in deep prayer in my bedroom. As my prayer intensified, I found myself power walking back and forth in the room. Suddenly, my pace was interrupted by the presence of something standing in front of me. I was afraid of what I might see when I opened my eyes. Yet, I was too curious to keep them shut. Before I could look however, I heard the Holy Spirit instruct me to feel the nature of what I had approached. So, I stood still, eyes closed and felt for it. Immediately, I knew it was not demonic! I was familiar with the presence of evil beings. I had been confronted by them before in prayer. On the contrary, this time was different. I felt such peace. Not only did I feel a spirit of security, I strangely sensed a belonging. I further questioned the Holy Spirit to give me clarity. I heard Him say, "*you have met your true covering in the spirit. You will likewise meet him in the natural. You will identify him by what you feel in this moment. He will be tall in stature and tall in the Kingdom of God.*" I held those words of hope in my heart although I did not know the extent of what they meant. I perceived that God was going to send someone to help cover the ministry. Later, I would learn that the mystery man was not going to just cover ministry, he was going to cover me.

By the end of consecration, I was laying prostrate before God in prayer. My heart was heavy because the enemy had once again shot the arrow of vindictiveness. I had received news of a person who was working to have our ministry's lease rescinded. Thoughts and questions flooded my mind. We had a sizable congregation of faithful followers. What would I do with them? Would God grace me to start ministry over again? If so, where would I go to start over? I did not want this to be another strike against those who were already broken because of my marital separation. As I cried out to Him from my bedroom floor, I felt the peace of God rest upon me and lift the weight of what I was carrying. I heard the spirit of the Lord say, "*you will not have to move nor will you have to fight in this. Be still. I am God.*" I wept with relief. As I got up from the floor, I heard another word of knowledge! *"Your divorce attorney will send for you and show you uncommon favor"*. In that moment, I realized divorce was going to be my reality. If God had told me that He was going to make my marriage new again, I would have waited and submitted to Him. However, beyond any doubt, I understood that my marriage had run its course. Within three days of hearing those words spoken, an attorney sent for me to come see him. He showed me uncommon favor. Within 3 months, I was divorced on the grounds of adultery.

Life has a way of throwing curve balls you never saw coming. Before I was divorced, I never envisioned myself as a divorcee. I thought a broken marriage was one of the worst things that could ever happen to me. After all, I was a pastor. Divorce was viewed as an unmentionable in the church community. But God had to allow me to see that I could live through it and recover from it. He was redirecting my whole life!

In hindsight, I know God used that season of my life to help me. I thought I would remain married forever, partly because I felt I needed to accept the responsibility and consequences of my decision. In addition, I did not want to feel like I failed. For years, I labored to keep an image before others by holding on to what was no longer conducive for the direction in which my life was moving. Like the items I had to part with during the deep cleaning of my home, the relationship had been worn by so many other things, it no longer fit me. I had to let it go and admit that old could no longer accommodate my new. Even though divorce was a blow to my pride, I needed to be broken there. Otherwise, pride may have been the stumbling block which would have prevented me from starting over. In some regard, it may have seemed easier to settle for what was. However, second best can never be as rewarding as living destiny's best!

Three years after my divorce, I literally married the man of my dreams. When I was around 12 years old, I had a recurring dream of a tall, handsome young man who would come to see me on an airplane. I was so in love with him. We would walk arm in arm. His smile was captivating. I would weep every time he had to leave me. The last time I saw him in my dream, I was about 14 years old. He promised me that he would come back and take me with him the next time. I never saw him in my dream again. It would be years later before a photograph would confirm the identity of my dream realm sweetheart.

I physically met him for the first time in a newly formed church. I was invited by the pastor to be their guest speaker. He was the minister on program to pray. At first, I did not notice him. I was nervous! But, the anointing on his life got my attention. He prayed and the Holy Ghost stood up inside of me! After the prayer, the powerful preacher walked up to me and apologized for having to leave. He explained that he had another engagement but told me to let the Lord use me. Just like that, he was gone. I ran into the mysterious minister several weeks later at the same church. That night, I was teaching a class. He sat with a nonchalant expression on his face the entire time. I started to assume that he was egotistical and did not fancy female preachers. Afterwards, the Holy Spirit instructed me to ask him to pray. At first, I was reluctant to do so. In my mind, I argued with God. "Why should I ask this stiff egotistical man to pray God? Anybody but him, please!" But eventually, I obeyed. As I stood before him to make my request, I gasped. It was like Deja vu. I was standing before a very tall man with feelings of peace, security, and a sense of belonging washing over me like waves. My tone softened, and I asked him to pray. He agreed. His smile melted the hardness of my heart! As he prayed, I laid hands on those at the altar call. The power of God was so intense. It felt like wind was at my back pushing me through the people. Over the next three years, he and I would go on to become best friends as we labored tirelessly to birth a new ministry together. Finally, we stood at the altar before our spiritual fathers in the gospel who united us in Holy Matrimony.

One marriage failed, but God gave me a new heart and a fresh start. He sent a beautiful king into my life to find me. He won me over with a song of unconditional love. Although I secretly felt unworthy at times, my husband loved me with the heart of the Lord and that made me sing! God blessed us with new love, new ministry, new business, and new family. He made all things new for us because we did not fight Him when it became necessary to change our song and our players. Beloved, God would be delighted to do the same for you. Psalms 35:27 New King James Versions *says Let them shout for joy and be glad, who favor my righteous cause; And let them say continually, "Let the LORD be magnified, Who has pleasure in the prosperity of His servants."* God is in favor of your prosperity. He only asks that you favor His righteousness by walking in it. He wants you to sing a prosperous song.

The reality is life brings change although most people despise it and find it hard to accept. Sometimes, we simply outgrow what once fit us perfectly. This includes, but is not limited to careers, relationships, mindsets, attitudes, outlooks, ambitions, needs, and desires. As much as we may prefer to keep things as they were, we cannot be afraid to expand when the opportunity presents itself. I know it is not always easy to move from what is familiar when it seems so safe. Familiar shows you clearly *what is* but uses fear to disguise what *could be*! Although the unfamiliar can be intimidating, the trip can also be exhilarating. Some of you may never know the excitement of a new thing because you are robbing yourself of the experience. If I could tap into the station of your soul right now, I would hear a song on repeat entitled "*But I am familiar with failure*"! It is time to switch the station! Do not sell yourself short because of what did not work before. Beloved, yesterday is gone, but today awaits. Get up, believe, and try again. You will never know what lies before you if you fail to forge your way into it. I have learned that we often cry over what we have lost because we could not perceive what we would gain. I am a firm believer that there were times in our lives when God did not allow the success of what we yearned for. Yet, He was faithful. Especially in the moments when He held us together as we watched our desired thing crumble. Let us thank His infinite wisdom. He knew that what we wanted was far less than what He had prepared for us. John 15:11 New Living Translation conveys the heart of the Lord towards His children. It says, "I *have told you these things so that you will be filled with my joy. Yes, your joy will overflow.*" God wants your joy to overflow. Did the thing that failed cause an abundant overflow of joy in your life? More than seventy five percent of you probably responded with a resounding NO! The old cliché says, "don't cry over spilled milk". Let there be no more tears of regret over what you have labeled "wasted" or "lost" in your life. It is time to take the sad song off repeat. You could be holding hands with your best years as you dance to a new beat. Put God as your top priority. Then, be relentless! Search until you find the perfect ballad of true fulfillment, even if you must write your own new song! You can have the relationship, the career, the degree, the ministry, the business, and the family. Joy, hope, love, peace, and great success can be yours. The list is never ending. It is all available to you. With the right focus, effort and fight, your song could be one of victory!

Have you ever heard a song that you did not like, but found yourself singing it anyway? For some of you, that has become a reflection of your existence. Your reality is not something that you hoped for. It is what you found yourself caught up in. Life can be amazingly beautiful one day, then reduced to the nonsense of confusing lyrics stuck in your head the next. I understand what it is like to struggle as you try to write the anthem of your life. Situations can leave you disoriented and at a loss for words. Disappointment might challenge your ability to stay on beat. Anger may cause you to jump key and sing in an off note for a while. Hurt will altogether strip you of your passion and reason to sing. Perhaps you can relate. If so, maybe God wants to change your tempo and give you new lyrics. It is easy to become programmed by routine and reject anything outside of your norm. However, you need to be open and receptive to new and different if that is what God has determined for your life. Please accept this truth, Beloved. Things seldom stay the same. Your life could begin as a melodious song with perfect harmony and without warning, plummet to a series of unwelcomed flat notes! Nevertheless, like a song, you do not have to continue to sing in error. Never be afraid to clear your throat and start again. In the music industry, there are people known as *one hit wonders*. However, I choose to believe that there is more than one single in you. Never stop composing! Inspire someone with your life's song!

Beloved, I stand in awe of God. He has given me new songs mixed with beautiful worship, ignited inspiration and exciting praise! With joy, I have chosen to sing again and again and again!

Among the many lessons life has taught, I have discovered that a new beginning is the result of an ending. The closing of one thing is often essential to the opening of another. Every conclusion does not always indicate finality. So even when it looks like it is over, stay tuned!

A redirected me!

He has given me a new song to sing, a hymn of praise to our God. Many will see what he has done and be amazed. They will put their trust in the Lord.
Psalms 40:3 NLT

Psalm 119:71 New International Version (NIV)

It was good for me to be afflicted
so that I might learn your decrees.

Made in the USA
Coppell, TX
02 August 2020